# AARON COPLAND
## Ballet Music for Piano

# CONTENTS

BOOSEY & HAWKES

AN IMAGEM COMPANY

DISTRIBUTED BY

HAL•LEONARD
CORPORATION
7777 W. BLUEMOUND RD. P.O. BOX 13819 MILWAUKEE, WI 53213

www.boosey.com
www.halleonard.com

# AARON COPLAND
## (1900-1990)

Aaron Copland's name is, for many, synonymous with American music. It was his pioneering achievement to break free from Europe and create a concert music that is recognizably, characteristically American. At the same time, he was able to stamp his music with a compositional personality so vivid as to transcend stylistic boundaries, making every work—from the easily-grasped to the demanding—identifiable as his alone.

From his early studies in piano he proceeded, at age 17, to study harmony, counterpoint, and sonata form with Rubin Goldmark, whose staunchly conservative outlook inspired Copland to rebellious investigation of the music of Debussy, Ravel, Mussorgsky, and Scriabin. In 1920, he set out for Paris, modernism's home in the years between the wars. Among the many vital legacies of his stay in Paris were his association with his teacher and mentor Nadia Boulanger; a growing interest in popular idioms; and the insight that there was as yet no American counterpart to the national styles being created by composers from France, Russia, and Spain. He became determined to create, in his words, "a naturally American strain of so-called serious music."

Upon his return to America in 1924, his career was launched when Serge Koussevitzky, whom he had met in Paris, agreed to conduct the Boston Symphony Orchestra in Copland's Organ Symphony, with Boulanger as soloist. When performed in New York under Walter Damrosch, the dissonant, angular work created a sensation. But Copland saw a broader role for himself than mere iconoclast. He sought to further the cause of new music as a vital cultural force. He accomplished this not only by composing, but also by lecturing and writing on new music, and by organizing the groundbreaking Copland-Sessions concerts in New York, which brought many works of the European avant-garde to U.S. audiences for the first time.

As America entered first a Depression, and then a war, Copland began to share many of his fellow artists' commitment to capturing a wider audience and speaking to the concerns of the average citizen in those times of trouble. His intentions were fulfilled as works from *Billy the Kid* to *Lincoln Portrait* to the Pulitzer Prize-winning *Appalachian Spring* found both popular success and critical acclaim. His decision to "say it in the simplest possible terms" alienated some of his peers, who saw in it a repudiation of musical progress—theirs and his own. But many who had been drawn to Copland's music through his use of familiar melodies were in turn perplexed by his use, beginning in the mid-1950's, of an individualized 12-tone compositional technique. His orchestral works *Connotations* (1962) and *Inscape* (1967) stand as perhaps the definitive statements of his mature, "difficult" style.

Copland never ceased to be an emissary and advocate of new music. In 1951, he became the first American composer to hold the position of Norton Professor of Poetics at Harvard University; his lectures there were published as *Music and Imagination*. For 25 years he was a leading member of the faculty at the Berkshire Music Center (Tanglewood). Throughout his career, he nurtured the careers of others, including Leonard Bernstein, Carlos Chávez, Toru Takemitsu, and David Del Tredici. He took up conducting while in his fifties, becoming a persuasive interpreter of his own music; he continued to conduct in concerts, on the radio, and on television until he was 83.

Aaron Copland was one of the most honored cultural figures in the history of the United States. The Presidential Medal of Freedom, the Kennedy Center Award, the National Academy of Motion Picture Arts and Sciences "Oscar", and the Commander's Cross of the Order of Merit of the Federal Republic of Germany were only a few of the honors and awards he received. In addition, he was president of the American Academy of Arts and Letters; a fellow of the Royal Academy of Music and the Royal Society of Arts in England; helped found the American Composers Alliance; was an early and prominent member of the American Society of Composers, Authors, and Publishers; served as director or board member of the American Music Center, the Koussevitzky Foundation, the League of Composers, and other organizations; received honorary doctorates from over 40 colleges and universities. In 1982, The Aaron Copland School of Music was established in his honor at Queens College of the City University of New York.

# NOTES FROM THE ORIGINAL PUBLICATIONS

## APPALACHIAN SPRING

This note appeared in the scores of the original chamber ensemble suite for 13 instruments, and the suite for symphony orchestra:

*Appalachian Spring* was composed in 1943–44 as a ballet for Miss Martha Graham on a commission from the Elisabeth Sprague Coolidge Foundation. It was first performed by Miss Graham and her company at the Coolidge Festival in the Library of Congress, Washington, D.C., on October 30, 1944.

The action of the ballet concerns "a pioneer celebration in spring around a newly-built farmhouse in the Pennsylvania hills in the early part of the last century [1800s]. The bride-to-be and the young farmer-husband enact the emotions, joyful and apprehensive, their new domestic partnership invites. An Older neighbor suggests now and then the rocky confidence of experience. A revivalist and his followers remind the new householders of the strange and terrible aspects of human fate. At the end the couple is left quiet and strong in their new house."

In 1945 *Appalachian Spring* received the Pulitzer Prize for music, as well as the award of the Music Critics Circle of New York for the outstanding theatrical work of the season of 1944–45.

*About Appalachian Spring Suite (solo piano transcription)*
The scores of the original version for 13 instrument chamber ensemble and the composer's 1945 suite for symphony orchestra were consulted in preparation of this solo piano transcription. This solo edition follows the musical form of the 1945 orchestral suite. All tempo indications and expressive markings have been retained, as have most articulations. Small, occasional adjustments have been made to create an idiomatic piano work. The pianist may choose to consult the study score of the orchestral suite for consideration of instrumental timbres.

## BILLY THE KID

This Suite is taken from the ballet *Billy the Kid* written for the American Ballet Caravan at the suggestion of its director Lincoln Kirstein and based on a story by Eugene Loring. The following is a quotation from an article by Aaron Copland "Notes on a Cowboy Ballet." "The action begins and closes on the open prairie. The central portion of the ballet concerns itself with significant moments in the life of Billy the Kid. The first scene is a street in a frontier town. Familiar figures amble by. Cowboys saunter into town, some on horseback, others with their lassos. Some Mexican women do a Jarabe which is interrupted by a fight between two drunks. Attracted by the gathering crowd, Billy is seen for the first time as a boy of twelve with his mother. The brawl turns ugly, guns are drawn, and in some unaccountable way, Billy's mother is killed. Without an instant's hesitation, in cold fury, Billy draws a knife from a cowhand's sheath and stabs his mother's slayers. His short but famous career had begun. In swift succession we see episodes in Billy's later life. At night, under the stars, in a quiet card game with his outlaw friends. Hunted by a posse led by his former friend Pat Garrett. Billy is pursued. A running gun battle ensues. Billy is captured. A drunken celebration takes place. Billy in prison is, of course, followed by one of Billy's legendary escapes. Tired and worn in the desert, Billy rests with his girl. (Pas de deux). Starting from a deep sleep, he senses movement in the shadows. The posse has finally caught up with him. It is the end."

## DANCE PANELS

### (Ballet in Seven Sections)

The first performance of *Dance Panels* was given by the Bavarian State Opera Ballet, Munich, on December 3, 1963, with choreography by Heinz Rosen, sets by Rudolph Heinrich, costumes by Charlotte Flemming and the composer conducting.

*Note on performance*
The music of the ballet was conceived as dance music, but without any specific 'story' in mind. The choreographer may present it as an 'abstract' ballet or as a 'story' ballet, according to his own ideas.

In concert performance, *Dance Panels* is to be played as one extended movement with only brief pauses between the separate sections.

Note that in ballet performances the fermata in the measure that precedes rehearsal numbers 1, 2, 3 and 8 is intended to last a considerable time during which the dance proceeds in silence. When performed in concert, however, each fermata should last for only the normal time span.

A.C.

# RODEO

## (Ballet in One Act)

The Ballet Russe de Monte Carlo commissioned the choreographer Agnes de Mille and the composer Aaron Copland to collaborate on the creation of a western ballet for its 1942-43 season. Originally sub-titled The Courting at Burnt Ranch, *Rodeo* was first produced at the Metropolitan Opera House on October 16, 1942 with scenery by Oliver Smith and costumes by Kermit Love.

The idea for the ballet was devised by Miss de Mille who described it as follows:

"Throughout the American Southwest, the Saturday afternoon rodeo is a tradition. On the remote ranches, as well as in the trading centers and the towns the 'hands' get together to show off their skill in roping, riding, branding and throwing. Often, on the more isolated ranches, the rodeo is done for an audience that consists only of a handful of fellow-workers, women-folk, and those nearest neighbors who can make the eighty or so mile run-over.

"The afternoon's exhibition is usually followed by a Saturday night dance at the Ranch House.

"The theme of the ballet is basic. It deals with the problem that has confronted all American women, from earliest pioneer times, and which has never ceased to occupy them throughout the history of the building of our country: how to get a suitable man."

The music was written in June, and orchestrated in September, 1942. The composer subsequently extracted an orchestral suite from the ballet score for concert performance under the title: *Four Dance Episodes from Rodeo*: I. Buckaroo Holiday, II. Corral Nocturne, III. Saturday Night Waltz, IV. Hoe-Down. A number of American folk songs are woven into the score. Source material was drawn from *Our Singing Country* by John A. and Alan Lomax and Ira Ford's *Traditional Music of America*. Two songs from the Lomax volume are incorporated into the first Episode: "If he'd be a buckaroo by his trade" and "Sis Joe." The rhythmic oddities of "Sis Joe" provided rich material for reworking. A square dance tune called "Bonyparte" provides the principal theme of the Hoe-Down. On the other hand no folk material was drawn upon for the Corral Nocturne.

Three Episodes were first performed in a concert by the Boston Pops Orchestra under Arthur Fiedler on May 28, 1943. The entire suite was premiered by Alexander Smallens at the Stadium Concerts with the New York Philharmonic Symphony in July 1943.

# DANCE OF THE ADOLESCENT

## (from *Dance Symphony*)

*Dance of the Adolescent* is an excerpt from *Grohg*, a ballet composed from 1922 to 1924, during the composer's student years in Paris. The story of the ballet tells of a magician, Grohg by name, who possessed the power to revive the dead and make them dance. In 1930, three dances were extracted from the ballet for symphonic performance under the title *Dance Symphony*. This won an RCA Victor prize of $5,000 in the same year. *Dance of the Adolescent* is the opening movement of the *Dance Symphony*. This arrangement for two pianos was made by the composer.

# APPALACHIAN SPRING SUITE
## (Ballet for Martha)

AARON COPLAND
(1943-1944)
Transcribed for piano solo
by Bryan Stanley

2

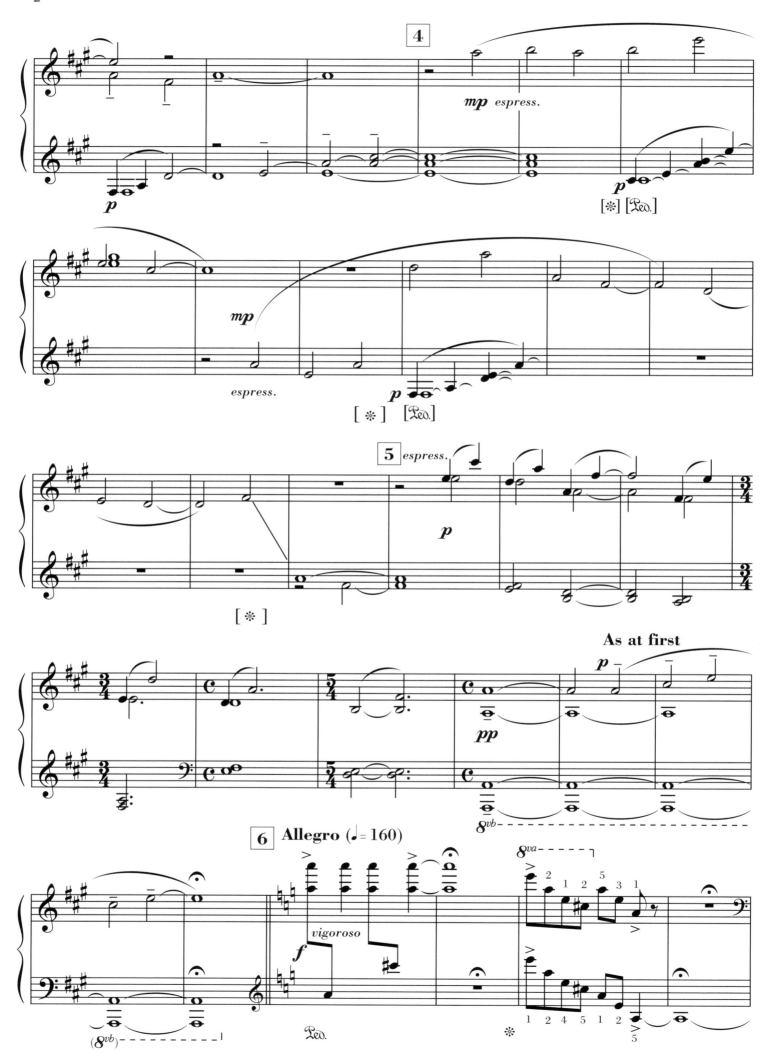

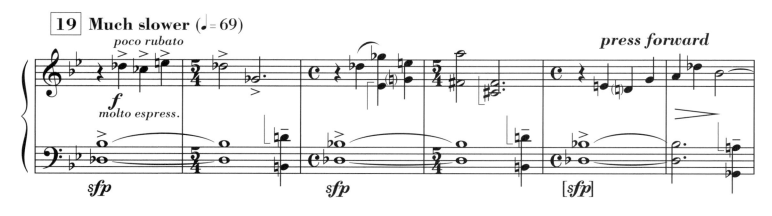

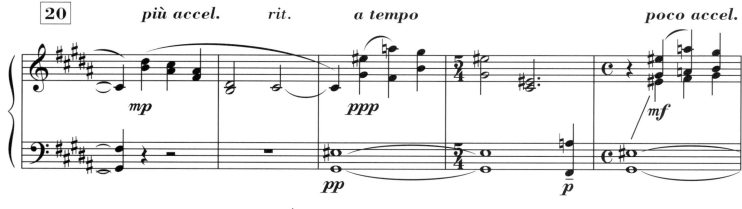

**28** More deliberate tempo (♩= 126)

* Shaker Melody: "The gift to be simple"

A trifle faster (♩= 80)

57

58

59

cantabile dolce, senza pedale

# BILLY THE KID
## Excerpts from the Ballet
### I. The Open Prairie

AARON COPLAND
(1938)
Arranged for piano solo
by Lukas Foss

## II. Street Scene in a Frontier Town
### A. Cowboys amble by

* Due to the quick tempo, the grace note in the left hand may be sounded simultaneously with the G.

## B. Mexican dance and finale

## III. Billy and His Sweetheart

## IV. Celebration after Billy's Capture

# DANCE PANELS
## (Ballet in Seven Sections)
### I.

AARON COPLAND
(1959, rev. 1962)

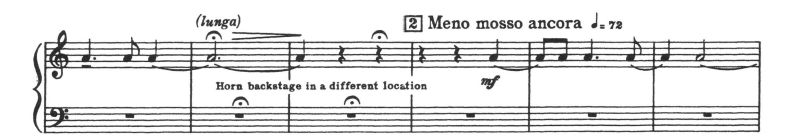

## II.

# III.

TRANSITION TO IV

44 Moderato ♩.=92

attacca

# IV.

# V.

# VI.

attacca

# VII.

CODA
**101** Come prima: espressivo, un poco rubato ♩ = 48

February-June 1959
Revised 1962

# RODEO
## Buckaroo Holiday

AARON COPLAND
(1942)

PIANO

89

98

# Corral Nocturne

100

# Ranch House Party

# Saturday-Night Waltz

## Hoe-Down

# DANCE OF THE ADOLESCENT
## (from *Dance Symphony*)

AARON COPLAND
(1933)